Pape

Written and Compiled by **Barbara F. Backer**
Illustrated by **Susan Simon**

Totline® Publications
A Division of Frank Schaffer Publications, Inc.
Torrance, California

Totline Publications would like to thank the following people for their contributions to this book: Lisa Blum, Del Rio, TX; Sarah Cooper, Arlington, TX; Colrain Pettipaw Hunley, Doylestown, PA; Susan M. Paprocki, Northbrook, IL; Kay Roozen, Des Moines, IA; Nancy C. Windes, Denver, CO.

Managing Editor: Kathleen Cubley
Contributing Editors: Carol Gnojewski, Susan Hodges, Elizabeth McKinnon, Susan Sexton, Jean Warren
Copyeditor: Kris Fulsaas
Proofreader: Miriam Bulmer
Editorial Assistant: Durby Peterson
Graphic Designer (Interior): Sarah Ness
Layout Artist: Gordon Frazier
Graphic Designer (Cover): Brenda Mann Harrison, Sarah Ness, Laura Horman
Production Manager: Melody Olney

Some of the ideas in this book may appear in other Totline® publications.

ISBN: 1-57029-229-9

Printed in the United States of America
Published by Totline Publications

Editorial Office: P.O. Box 2250
                       Everett, WA 98203
Business Office: 23740 Hawthorne Blvd.
                       Torrance, CA 90505

20 19 18 17 16 15 14 13 12 11 10 9 8 7 6 5 4 3 2 1

Introduction

Paper is all around us. We take it for granted. But this "throwaway" substance can be a powerful learning tool that's lots of fun, too.

When children make something from paper, they learn that one object (paper) can be used to represent another (airplane, hat, hair). When they fold paper, cut it, or glue pieces of it together to form another object, they learn about how a material can retain some of its characteristics while other characteristics change. When folding a rectangle of paper into a square, or a circle into quarters, children learn about beginning geometry and fractions.

Paper is divided into ten sections: "Construction Paper," "Paper Sacks," "Newspapers," "Paper Plates," "Envelopes," "Wallpaper & Gift Wrap," "Paper Shapes," "Index Cards," "Fast-Food Containers," and "Kitchen Papers." On each page you will find an activity that your child can do alone or one that you can do together.

Many of the activities use types of paper that serve a functional use in your life—paper sacks, newspaper, paper plates, index cards, gift wrap, envelopes. Using these types of paper helps children understand that one item can have various uses. While enjoying the activities, children learn how to recycle previously used items.

Most pages include a hint to make the activity easier. In addition, under the heading "For More Fun" you'll find suggestions for varying the activity. You can help your child develop creative thinking skills by encouraging him or her to think of additional things to do with the materials.

A Word About Safety—All of the activities in this book are appropriate for 3- to 5-year-olds. However, it is important that an adult supervise the activities to make sure that children do not put any materials or objects in their mouth. As for art materials, such as scissors, glue, or felt tip markers, use those that are specifically labeled as safe for children unless the materials are to be used only by an adult.

Contents

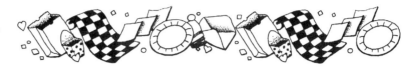

Your child will enjoy this activity's almost magical results.

Sun Prints

You Will Need
- ○ dark construction paper
- ○ everyday items

Have your child set pieces of dark construction paper in direct sunlight. Let him arrange everyday items, such as blocks, pencils, and toy cars, on the papers. Ask him to predict what will happen as the sun shines on the papers all day long.

At the end of the day, have him remove the items and observe what has happened to the papers. Which parts are lighter than the others? Why? (Sunlight bleaches the exposed paper. The original color remains in areas not exposed to sunlight.)

Hint: Save this activity for a bright, sunny day. Place the papers where they'll receive strong, direct sunlight and leave them for at least several hours.

For More Fun: Place some transparent items (clear drinking glass, clear-plastic plate) on the papers along with the solid, opaque objects. What happens? Discuss the results with your child.

*Making gifts for the entire
family will give your child a thrill.*

Special-Occasion Placemats

You Will Need

O construction paper

O stickers

O markers

Give your child a piece of construction paper for each family member. Let her decorate the paper by applying stickers or drawing with markers. Put each family member's name on his or her placemat.

Hint: To make the placemats more durable, cover them on both sides with clear self-stick paper. Covered mats hold up when cleaned with a damp cloth.

For More Fun: Have each family member make a personalized placemat.

*Your child can enjoy making
and reading a book of his own.*

Color Book

Help your child make a book by stapling several sheets of white paper together with a construction paper cover. For a book about the color red, use a red cover.

Let your child find and cut out magazine or catalog pictures that are red. Have him glue one picture to each page. Using a red marker, label each page "red truck," "red apple," etc.

Hint: Don't be concerned if there are several colors in the pictures your child selects. Have him draw an arrow on the page pointing to the red part of his selected picture.

For More Fun: Help your child make a book about each of the six colors in the rainbow. Encourage him to read the book to family members.

Your child will feel like
royalty in this birthday hat.

Birthday Hat

You Will Need
- ○ child-safe scissors
- ○ ruler
- ○ construction paper
- ○ glue
- ○ tape

Help your child cut out a 3-inch-wide construction paper strip that is long enough to fit around her head. Have her cut the appropriate number of candle shapes out of different colors of construction paper, and add a matching number of yellow flames.

Wrap the long strip around her head and mark the center front. Have her glue the candles onto the top of the strip near the center front, and glue the flames onto the candles.

Write "Happy Birthday" and your child's name below the candles. Adjust the hat to fit your child's head and secure it with tape.

Hint: Don't worry about having your child cut a straight hat and neat candles. She will enjoy this hat because she made it herself.

For More Fun: Make similar hats for other special occasions.

This guessing game is fun to play again and again.

What Is It?

You Will Need
○ scissors
○ paper lunch bags
○ stapler
○ markers

Cut 2 inches off the tops of several paper lunch bags that you have left folded flat. Stack the bags on top of one another with all the flaps folded on the right. Then staple the bags together on the left-hand side to make a book.

Use markers to draw a picture under each flap so that part of the picture is visible when the flap is closed. As your child looks through the book, have him look at the part of each picture that is showing and try to predict what is hidden beneath the flap before lifting it up.

Hint: Older children like to make these books for their younger siblings.

For More Fun: Instead of drawing a picture, glue a cut-out magazine picture under each flap, or make photocopies of family snapshots and glue a copy under each flap.

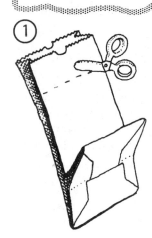

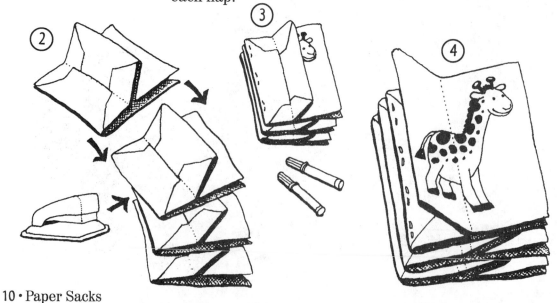

Your child can use this little basket to store small treasures.

Sack Basket

You Will Need
- paper lunch bag
- scissors
- crayons, markers, or stickers
- stapler or glue

Help your child make an instant basket by folding a paper lunch bag in half lengthwise. Form a handle by rounding off the top corner and cutting out the middle of the bag, as shown in the illustration.

Encourage your child to decorate her basket with crayons, markers, or stickers. When it is decorated, staple or glue the handles together.

Hint: Encourage your child to make these baskets often. They can be used to pick up small treasures, such as rocks and leaves, when you go for a walk.

For More Fun: Perhaps your child would like to line the basket with facial tissues to form a portable bed for her small dolls, stuffed animals, or action figures.

It's always fun to try a new hairstyle!

Paper-Bag Wig

You Will Need
- ○ scissors
- ○ large brown paper grocery bag
- ○ pencil

Show your child how to make a wig by cutting a large rectangle from the front section of a large brown paper grocery bag, leaving about 2 inches on the sides and bottom of the bag. Turn the bag upside down and cut a fringe around the open end of the bag. Help your child curl the fringe by tightly rolling each section around a pencil and holding it there for a few seconds.

Let your child put on the wig and check out his new identity in a mirror!

For More Fun: Your child may want to make a fancy hat from construction paper to glue on top of his new hairdo.

Your child will enjoy flying this kite on a windy day.

Bag Kites

You Will Need
- ○ small paper bag
- ○ crayons or markers
- ○ hole punch
- ○ yarn

Have your child decorate a small paper bag with crayons or markers. Punch a hole on the top side of the bag near the opening and tie a piece of yarn through the hole. When your child holds the string and runs, the "kite" will fill with air and fly up and down behind her.

Hint: You can reinforce the string hole by covering the area with layers of masking tape before you punch the hole.

For More Fun: Try this as a birthday-party activity, then have the children fly their kites outside.

Develop your child's creative thinking skills when you do this activity together.

Writing Stories

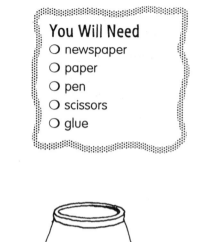

You Will Need
- O newspaper
- O paper
- O pen
- O scissors
- O glue

Sit down with your child and look at a picture in a newspaper. Ask your child to tell you a story about what he sees. On a piece of paper, write down exactly what your child says. Cut out the picture. Then glue the picture and the story onto a larger piece of paper and display it in your home (perhaps on the refrigerator).

At first your child may tell you one short sentence like "That's a man" or "He's kicking a football," but each time you repeat the activity, his "stories" will grow.

Hint: Younger children may just "label" parts of the picture, pointing and saying things like "lady," "eye," "arm," "pocketbook." Write those words on the paper and draw arrows to the places your child pointed to.

For More Fun: Put the date on each story. Save the stories in a binder for your child to look at and "read" again and again. Over time you will see your child's growth as you look at the stories.

Your child will enjoy dancing to music while she waves these pompoms.

Pompoms

You Will Need
O child-size scissors
O ruler
O newspaper
O stapler

Help your child cut 2-foot lengths of newspaper strips approximately 2 inches wide. Stack ten of the strips together and staple them at one end to make a pompom. Your child can use these while moving to music, while running with the pompoms waving behind like streamers, and while pretending to be a cheerleader.

For More Fun: You and your child can make similar pompoms from crepe paper or from plastic-bag strips. Invite your child's friends to make pompoms with you, then hold an impromptu cheerleading party.

This hat can be made
quickly for any occasion.

Happy Hat

You Will Need
○ newspaper
○ tape
○ stickers

Help your child fold a 24-by-28-inch piece of newspaper in half crosswise. Fold it in half again. With the second fold at the top, fold over the two sides of the paper so that they meet in the middle, forming a triangle. Fold up the bottom edges of the paper twice to make a hat rim, and secure the edges with tape. Have your child decorate the hat with brightly colored stickers.

Hint: Use the comic section for a whimsical, colorful hat.

For More Fun: When your child and his friends all make Happy Hats, they can march together and have a parade. Kitchen implements make good rhythm instruments.

*Help your child develop
a lifelong love of reading.*

Read All About It!

You Will Need
○ newspaper

With your child, go through the pages of a newspaper. Begin with one section. Show her the weather report and talk about the forecast for tomorrow's weather. Show her pictures and, in a simple way, tell her what they are about.

Each time you read the paper together, revisit places you've already looked at and add one or two more. If your child remains interested, show her where to find the grocery ads, clothing ads, the comic section, or local human-interest stories.

For More Fun: Some children are fascinated by the birth announcements and the death notices. Your child may want to count these each day and see whether there were more births or deaths announced that day.

Your child practices his counting skills with this game.

Counting Game

You Will Need
- marker
- paper plate
- dried beans

With a marker, divide a paper plate into four to eight triangular sections. Number the sections, starting with 1. Give your child some dried beans to use as counting objects. Sit with your child as he identifies each number and counts out the corresponding number of beans to place on each section.

Hint: Divide the plate into fewer sections for younger children, more sections for older ones. For younger children, in addition to the numerals, draw the correct number of dots in each section. Children who do not yet recognize numerals can match beans to dots.

For More Fun: You can substitute buttons, O-shaped cereal, or any similar item for the beans.

*Your child won't be puzzled
about why this activity is fun.*

Puzzle Plate

You Will Need
○ markers
○ paper plates
○ scissors

Help your child use a marker to color the rim of a paper plate. Let her draw a picture on the plate. Cut the plate into three to six puzzle pieces so no two are exactly alike. Give your child the puzzle pieces and a plain paper plate to use as a base. Challenge her to put her puzzle together.

Hint: A general guideline is to cut homemade puzzles into the number of pieces that corresponds to your child's age.

For More Fun: Have your child make more puzzle plates using leftover birthday-party plates that are decorated with cartoon or movie characters.

Sew up a lot of fun with this
hand-eye coordination activity!

Lacing Card

Help your child use a hole punch to make holes around the edge of a paper plate. Tie one end of a shoelace through one of the holes, and knot it securely. Let your child thread the shoelace in and out of the remaining holes.

Hint: Don't be concerned about whether your child sews "neatly." The important thing is getting the lace in and out of the holes.

For More Fun: Make lacing cards from the fronts of greeting cards, and use colorful yarn to lace them. Add a yarn loop to the cards and hang them up as decorations.

*Your child will have a
roaring good time with this mask.*

Leopard Mask

You Will Need
- child-safe scissors
- paper plate
- yellow paint
- paintbrush
- black marker or paint
- glue
- construction paper
- craft stick

Cut eye holes out of a paper plate. Have your child paint the back of the plate yellow. When the paint has dried, have her use a black marker or black paint to make the leopard's spots. Have her glue on nose and ear shapes she's cut from construction paper.

Attach a craft stick handle so your child can hold the mask in front of her face.

Hint: To eliminate the painting, begin with a yellow paper plate.

For More Fun: Experiment to make other animal masks. For instance, for a zebra mask, have your child use black markers to make stripes on a white paper plate. Then she'll add the nose and ear shapes and white or black paper strips around the plate's rim.

*Your child will enjoy playing
with this easy-to-make puppet.*

Perky Puppet

You Will Need
- O business-size envelope
- O markers

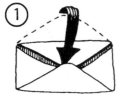

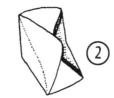

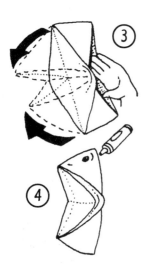

Help your child tuck in the flap of a business-size envelope. Have him place his hand inside the envelope with his fingers at one end and his thumb at the other. Indent the middle of the envelope toward his hand and show him how to fold his fingers and thumb together to make the puppet's mouth. Have him use markers to draw on facial features. Show him how to open and close his hand to make the puppet "talk."

Hint: For colorful puppets, use envelopes from junk mail.

For More Fun: Encourage your child to make animal puppets by adding construction paper ears and noses and drawing on fur with the markers.

These tiny baskets make great gifts.

Heart Basket

Help your child cut heart shapes out of the bottom corners of envelopes, as shown. Cut strips out of construction paper. Let your child decorate the heart shapes and paper strips with markers, crayons, or stickers. Help your child staple the strips to the heart shapes to create Heart Baskets. Your child can fill these special love baskets with tiny treats and deliver them to friends or family members.

Hint: Save brightly colored envelopes from greeting cards to use for the baskets.

For More Fun: Love knows no season. Make and use these baskets year-round.

Your child builds observation and thinking skills while playing this game.

Picture Flaps

You Will Need
- ○ scissors
- ○ large manila envelope
- ○ magazine or newspaper pictures

Cut four or five flaps in the front of a large manila envelope. Slide a colorful magazine or newspaper picture into the envelope, with the picture facing the flaps. Have your child open up one flap and let him try to guess what the picture is. Let him continue opening the flaps, one at a time, until he guesses correctly. Then pull out the picture for him to see, and replace it with another picture.

Hint: Hide the envelope while you change the pictures.

For More Fun: Place family photos in the envelope and try to identify the people by opening the flaps.

*Your child practices logical thinking and
learns math skills when she plays this game.*

Arranging Envelopes

You Will Need
○ variety of envelopes

Give your child a stack of various-sized envelopes,
and ask her to place the largest one on a flat surface.
One at a time, have her place the remaining envelopes
on top of the first one, arranging them from largest to
smallest.

Hint: Be certain that the envelopes are not close
in size.

For More Fun: Play this game when you are standing in
line at the post office. Have your child place the pieces
of mail in order on your outstretched hands.

Your child will sharpen visual skills while he matches mittens.

Mitten Match

You Will Need

- ○ mitten pattern cut from index card
- ○ pencil
- ○ child-safe scissors
- ○ variety of wallpaper or gift wrap scraps

Show your child how to trace mitten shapes. Have him trace mitten pairs on various kinds of wallpaper or gift wrap scraps. Help him cut out the mittens. Now, let him mix up the shapes, then find matching pairs.

Hint: Use paper that has a regular, even pattern like narrow stripes or small flowers. Cutting from randomly patterned paper doesn't always yield exact pattern matches. After drawing around the pattern one time, flip it over to draw the mitten's mate.

For More Fun: Hang a piece of thick yarn between two chairs. Provide small clothespins and encourage your child to clip the mittens, in pairs, to the "clothesline."

*Your child can capture
nature's beauty with this activity.*

Leafy Branches

You Will Need

O crayon
O construction paper
O child-safe scissors
O wallpaper or
  gift wrap scraps
O glue

Have your child use a crayon to draw a tree branch on a piece of white or light blue construction paper. Help her cut small leaf shapes from the wallpaper or gift wrap scraps and glue them on the tree branch.

Hint: To help your child become observant of nature's changes, do this activity at different seasons of the year. Together, observe the trees to see whether they are fully covered or scarcely covered with leaves.

For More Fun: Have your child cut flower shapes from the wallpaper or gift wrap scraps and glue them to light-colored construction paper. Let her add stems and leaves with a crayon.

A variety of squares and patterns make up this quilt.

Wallpaper Quilt

You Will Need
- ○ construction paper
- ○ ruler
- ○ scissors
- ○ wallpaper or gift wrap
- ○ glue

Fold a 9-inch square of construction paper into small squares. Cut wallpaper or gift wrap into matching-size squares. Encourage your child to glue the wallpaper squares onto the squares of the paper, making a "patch-work quilt."

Hint: Children with strong cutting skills can cut their own small squares of paper.

For More Fun: Instead of wallpaper or gift wrap, cut the fronts of old greeting cards into squares.

This activity helps your child see how different parts combine to make a whole.

Butterfly Puzzle

You Will Need
- child-safe scissors
- large sheet of wallpaper or gift wrap
- glue
- file folder

Help your child cut a large butterfly shape out of wallpaper or gift wrap. Glue this to a file folder half. When the glue dries, cut the butterfly into three or four puzzle pieces. Encourage your child to put the butterfly back together.

Hint: Store the puzzle pieces together in a resealable plastic bag.

For More Fun: Make a variety of similar puzzles from simple shapes such as hearts, trees, and circles.

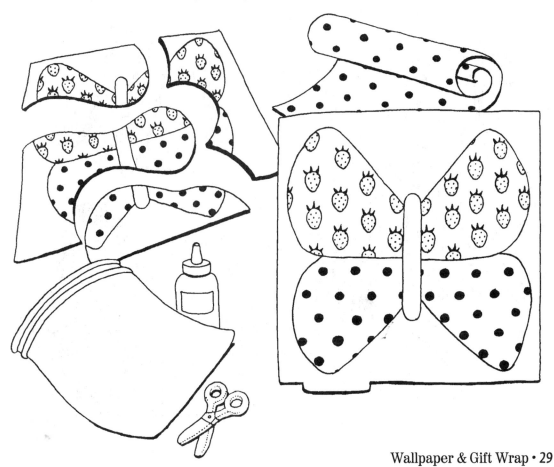

Your child will learn math skills while he makes and reads his very own book.

Simple Counting Book

You Will Need
- O stapler
- O white paper
- O construction paper
- O marker
- O scissors
- O glue
- O assorted paper shapes

Help your child make a book by stapling together ten pieces of white paper with a construction paper cover. Write "My Counting Book" and his name on the cover. Number the pages from 1 to 10. Purchase (or cut from construction paper) 55 small paper shapes. Help your child identify the numeral on each page and glue on the corresponding number of shapes.

Hint: For younger children, use only five pages and place the corresponding number of dots beside each numeral.

For More Fun: Encourage your child to make up a story for each page of shapes.

Your child can increase her memory skills when you play this game together.

Memory Game

You Will Need
- ○ scissors
- ○ construction paper

Cut three or four shapes from construction paper. Arrange the paper shapes on a table in front of your child. Have her close her eyes while you remove one of the shapes. After she opens her eyes, sing the following song and then have her guess which shape is missing.

There Is One

Sung to: "Frère Jacques"

There is one, there is one

Shape gone, shape gone.

Can you tell me which one,

Can you tell me which one

Is gone, is gone?

Gayle Bittinger

Hint: Start with just a few shapes. As your child's skill increases, add another shape or two.

For More Fun: Sometimes it's fun to remove two shapes at the same time. Let your child remove a shape or two while you hide your eyes.

With this activity, your child builds small muscles in his fingers.

Star Colors

You Will Need
- markers
- large paper star
- cardboard
- clear self-stick paper
- scissors
- wooden spring-type clothespins

Use markers to color each tip of a large paper star a different color. Attach the star to a piece of cardboard, cover it with clear self-stick paper, and trim the edges. Then color the ends of five wooden spring-type clothespins to match the colors on the star points.

Encourage your child to clip the clothespins to the matching star points.

Hint: Have your child name the color as he clips on the clothespin. If your child is just learning color names, provide the name for him.

For More Fun: You can turn this into a game by taking turns with your child while each of you clips clothespins onto your own stars.

Your child will think she's producing
magic when she makes these pictures.

Shape Rubbings

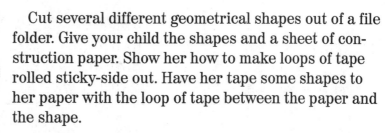

You Will Need
- ○ scissors
- ○ file folder
- ○ construction paper
- ○ tape
- ○ peeled crayon

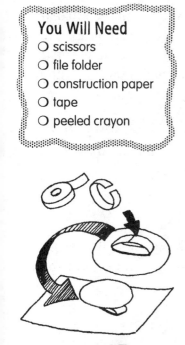

Cut several different geometrical shapes out of a file folder. Give your child the shapes and a sheet of construction paper. Show her how to make loops of tape rolled sticky-side out. Have her tape some shapes to her paper with the loop of tape between the paper and the shape.

Show your child how to use the side of a peeled crayon to rub over her shape, rubbing from the center of the shape toward and beyond the outside edges. Have her cover her paper with color. Then encourage her to remove her shapes to see what she has made.

Hint: A "chubby" crayon is easier for small hands to control.

For More Fun: After your child has made several pages of these shape pictures, have her try to match paper shapes to the outlines in her pictures.

*Your child develops reasoning
skills while he plays this game.*

Matching Game

Select five index cards and draw a simple picture, such as a circle, a star, a heart, a tree, or a triangle, in the center of each one. Help your child cut the cards in half and mix them up. Now encourage him to find the cards that match and put them together again.

Hint: For an additional challenge, add more cards.

For More Fun: Make a set of cards using pictures from magazines or from grocery ads.

Your child will become familiar with letters and their sounds with this unique book.

Accordion Book

You Will Need
- large index cards
- clear tape
- markers or crayons

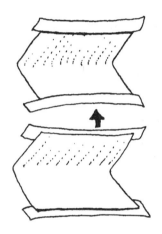

With your child, fold 13 large index cards in half. Unfold the cards and use clear tape to fasten them together end to end. (Tape both sides of the cards for a more durable book.) Use markers or crayons to label the sections on the cards from "A" to "Z." On each section, have your child draw a picture of something that begins with the letter that is printed on it. Fold the cards together accordion style. Encourage your child to "read" this book to family members and friends.

Hint: Making this book is a big project that can extend over several weeks. Let your child set the pace. Encourage her to draw pictures that interest her. When she can't think of an item she can draw for a particular letter, look together at alphabet books from the library for ideas. Pages can be completed in any order. Let your child work on pages that interest her.

For More Fun: Have other family members or friends draw pictures on empty pages. Use magazine or catalog pictures for some of the pages.

*Your child will love playing
this game with family or friends.*

Color Dominoes

Trim ten index cards to measure 2½ by 5 inches each. Draw a horizontal line across the middle of each card. Select five different rubber stamps and stamp a different design on each half of each card, as shown in the illustration below. Let your child lay out the cards so that the matching designs are touching, either vertically or horizontally.

For More Fun: Make this a family game. Using one or two more stamps, make additional dominoes. Place one domino on the table and deal remaining dominoes to players. In turn, each player adds a domino to either end of the domino "train" on the table. Any player who doesn't have a match misses a turn.

Sharpen observation and reasoning skills with this game.

Same and Different Cards

On a set of four index cards, encourage your child to draw pictures that are alike in some way (a red apple, a red car, a red heart, a red balloon, etc.). Make two additional four-card sets.

To play, lay out three cards containing pictures that are alike and one card containing a picture that is different. Ask your child to identify the different picture and to explain why it doesn't belong with the other three. Continue the game using combinations with the other cards.

Hint: Invite family members to make a set of cards and to join in the game.

This toy provides lots of fun and surprises.

Pop-up Puppet

Have your child cut a small face shape out of heavy paper and draw on facial features. Help him staple the face shape onto the top of a straw. Poke a hole in the bottom of a large cardboard French fry holder. With the holder upright, help your child stick the straw down into the holder, through the hole. Show your child how to move the straw up and down to make the puppet appear and disappear.

For More Fun: Make an entire family of pop-up puppets, including the family pets. These are great toys to use while riding in the car.

Your child will love talking to this funny-looking puppet.

Big Mouth Puppet

You Will Need
- ○ scissors
- ○ cardboard fast-food container
- ○ plastic moving eyes
- ○ marker

Cut the fastener tabs off a cardboard fast-food holder. Glue two plastic moving eyes on the front of the holder and add a mouth with a black marker. Carefully poke two finger holes in the back of the puppet, one in the lid and one in the bottom. To use the puppet, poke your index finger through the hole in the lid and your thumb through the hole in the bottom. Move your finger and thumb to open and close the puppet's mouth. Let your child try working the puppet, too.

Even the youngest child can build
reading skills when he "reads" this book!

Restaurant Book

You Will Need
- ○ white paper
- ○ stapler
- ○ construction paper
- ○ child-safe scissors
- ○ fast-food restaurant bags
- ○ glue

Help your child make a book by gathering several sheets of white paper and stapling them together with a construction paper cover. Have your child cut the logos from fast-food restaurant bags. Let him glue one logo to each page. When the glue dries, he'll enjoy "reading" his book.

For More Fun: Have your child make similar books using logos of other familiar businesses.

*Your child will enjoy making
a bouquet of these flowers.*

Paper-Cup Flower

You Will Need
○ child-safe scissors
○ paper cup
○ pencil
○ crayons, markers,
  or stickers
○ green pipe cleaner

Have your child make eight cuts in a paper cup from the rim to 1 inch from the bottom. To make flower petals, have her curl each strip out and down, wrapping it around a short pencil, then removing the pencil. Have her decorate the flower with crayons, markers, or stickers. Help her poke a green pipe cleaner through the bottom of the cup for a stem.

Hint: Display the completed flowers in a vase.

For More Fun: Use a variety of colorful cups for a bright bouquet.

*Help your child gain an appreciation
of the variety of leaves in your area.*

Aluminum-Foil Leaves

You Will Need
○ variety of leaves
○ aluminum foil
○ glue
○ construction paper

Collect a variety of leaves. Let your child select a leaf, place it under a piece of foil, and gently press and rub the foil with his hand to get a leaf print. Have him glue his print to a piece of construction paper.

Hint: Thick leaves are easiest to work with.

For More Fun: Make a variety of prints and hang them all together as a nature display. With help from library books, help your child learn the names of the trees whose leaves he has pressed. Label each print.

*Your young scientist can watch
seeds sprout and see roots develop.*

Seed-Viewing Jar

Help your child line a glass jar with two or three wet, solid-colored paper towels. Crumple up more wet paper towels and stuff them into the jar to hold the outer towels in place. Let your child fill the jar with 1 inch of water. Have her place dried beans between the paper towels and the jar. Place the jar in a warm, dark place. Take the jar out daily to observe the seeds. Add water as needed to keep it at the 1-inch level.

Hint: Mung beans and lima beans sprout quickly. When the jar begins to get moldy, it's time to throw it away.

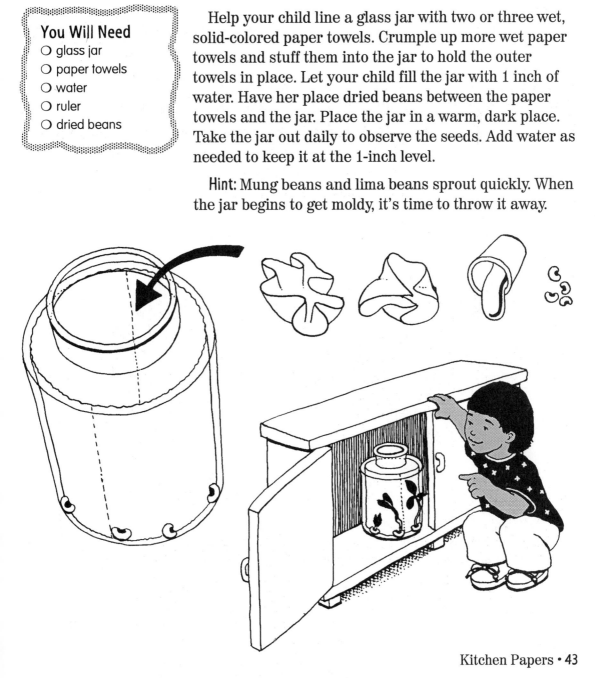

These textured papers
make a touchable collage.

Kitchen Collage

You Will Need
- O variety of kitchen papers
- O child-safe scissors
- O glue
- O dark-colored construction paper

Collect a variety of kitchen papers such as waxed paper, paper towels, paper napkins, freezer paper, and paper bags. Have your child cut or tear the papers into small pieces. Let him glue these to dark construction paper to make a textured kitchen collage.

For More Fun: Let your child add silvery aluminum foil pieces to make an icy-looking collage.

Entertain your child when
waiting in a restaurant.

Napkin Puppet

You Will Need
O paper napkin
O pen

Show your child how to slip her hand inside a paper napkin and bend her hand in half to create a puppet mouth. Have her add facial features with a pen. When she makes an additional puppet for you, your puppets can "talk" to one another.

For More Fun: When your child invites a friend for lunch, have her show the friend how to make a Napkin Puppet. You'll be entertained when the puppets talk to each other.

Parent Resources
from Totline® Publications

A Year of Fun

Hang up these age-specific resource guides for great advice on child development, practical parenting, and age-appropriate activities that jump-start learning.

• **Just for Babies**
• **Just for Ones**
• **Just for Twos**
• **Just for Threes**
• **Just for Fours**
• **Just for Fives**

Beginning Fun With Science

Make science fun for your child with these quick, safe, easy-to-do activities that lead to discovery and spark the imagination.

• **Bugs & Butterflies** • **Plants & Flowers**
• **Magnets** • **Rainbows & Colors**
• **Sand & Shells** • **Water & Bubbles**

Beginning Fun With Art

Perfect for introducing a young child to the fun of art while developing coordination skills and building self-confidence.

• **Scissors** • **Yarn** • **Paint** • **Modeling Dough**
• **Glue** • **Stickers** • **Craft Sticks** • **Crayons** • **Felt**
• **Paper Shapes** • **Rubber Stamps** • **Tissue Paper**

Learning Everywhere

These books present ideas for turning ordinary moments into teaching opportunities. You'll find ways to spend fun, quality time with your child while you lay the foundation for language, art, science, math, problem solving, and building self-esteem.

• **Teaching House**
• **Teaching Town**
• **Teaching Trips**

Getting Ready for School

Help your child develop the skills necessary for school success. These activity ideas combine ordinary materials with simple instructions for fun at home that leads to learning.

• **Ready to Learn Colors, Shapes, and Numbers**
• **Ready to Write and Develop Motor Skills**
• **Ready to Read** • **Ready to Communicate**
• **Ready to Listen and Explore the Senses**

Totline books and resources are available at fine teacher and parent stores.

Parent Resources
from Totline® Publications

Seeds for Success

Ideas on how to plant the seeds for success in young children. These parent-friendly books help encourage the development of creativity, responsibility, critical thinking, happiness, and good health. For ages 3 to 5.

- **Growing Creative Kids**
- **Growing Responsible Kids**
- **Growing Happy Kids**
- **Growing Thinking Kids**

Time to Learn

Now's the time for hands-on learning. Find out how to use low- and no-cost materials to effectively and simply teach your child at home.

- **Colors • Letters**
- **Measuring • Numbers**
- **Science • Shapes**
- **Matching and Sorting**
- **New Words**
- **Cutting and Pasting**
- **Drawing and Writing**
- **Listening**
- **Taking Care of Myself**

Learn With Piggyback® Songs

Children will love to learn age-appropriate themes through music and movement with these delightful song books. Each book has 40 joyful songs and rhymes that help children learn about a specific topic. Plus developmentally appropriate activity ideas extend the learning fun!

- **Songs and Games for Babies**
- **Songs and Games for Toddlers**
- **Songs and Games for Threes**
- **Songs and Games for Fours**
- **Sing a Song of Letters**
- **Sing a Song of Animals**
- **Sing a Song of Colors**
- **Sing a Song of Holidays**
- **Sing a Song of Me**
- **Sing a Song of Nature**
- **Sing a Song of Numbers**
- **Sing a Song of Shapes**

Cassette Tapes

Cassette tapes, featuring selected songs from some of the Learn with Piggyback Songs books, include:

- **Songs for Babies**
- **Songs for Toddlers**
- **Songs for Threes**
- **Songs for Fours**

Totline books and resources are available at fine teacher and parent stores.

Parent Resources
from Totline® Publications

Learn With Stickers

Use stickers to teach beginning colors, numbers, reading, and writing. Children can turn each workbook into a personalized storybook to keep and share. While an adult reads the book, children add stickers to complete the illustration on each page. Each interactive story provides practice in beginning reading and writing, counting, and identifying colors. More than 100 stickers included. Each 32 pages.

- **Balloons**
- **Birds**
- **Bows**
- **Bugs**
- **Butterflies**
- **Buttons**
- **Eggs**
- **Flags**
- **Flowers**
- **Hearts**
- **Leaves**
- **Mittens**

More than 100 stickers in each book!

7" x 9" size

Play & Learn

Learning through play the Totline way!

Each book in this delightful series focuses on a specific topic and introduces activities for using common objects in learning games and ideas for make-your-own projects. **Play & Learn** books are ideal resources for parents of ages 3 to 5.

- **Blocks**
- **Instruments**
- **Kitchen Gadgets**
- **Paper**
- **Puppets**
- **Puzzles**

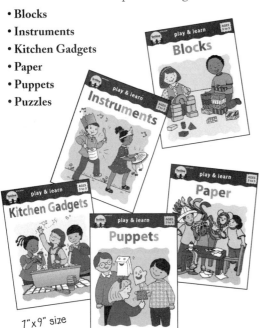

7" x 9" size

Let your child make a personalized storybook!

Totline books and resources are available at fine teacher and parent stores.